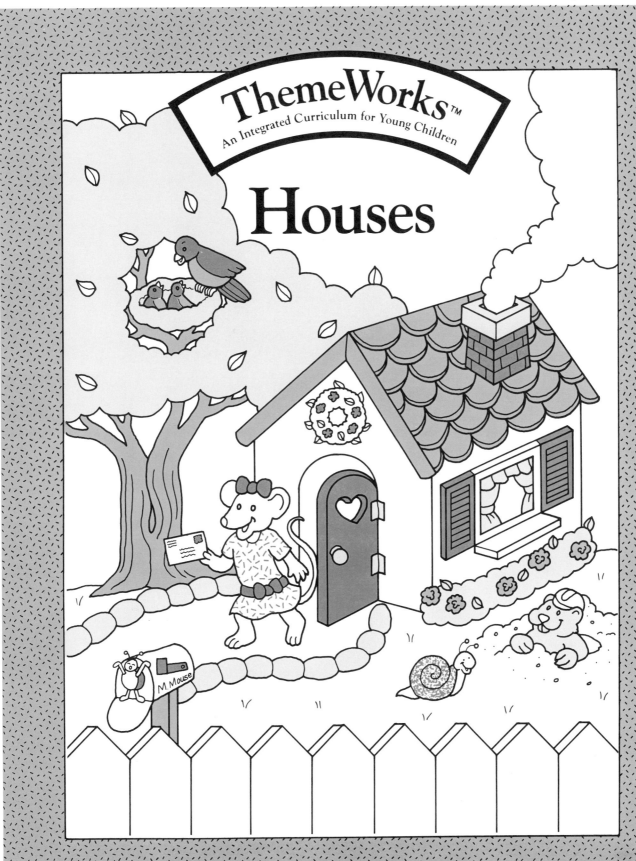

ThemeWorks™
An Integrated Curriculum for Young Children

Houses

Joan Westley
Illustrated by Elaine Abe

Creative
Publications

THEMEWORKS™: HOUSES

Creative Publications is a registered trademark.

With special thanks to Betsy Verne Franco and Holly Melton.

Grateful acknowledgement is made to the teachers and children who tried these materials in their classrooms:

Marlene Getz ◆ Berkeley, California
Kathleen Hammer ◆ Mountain View, California
Becky Kenfield ◆ Missoula, Montana
Kathy Muench ◆ Schaumberg, Illinois
Carolyn Nuite ◆ San Francisco, California
Claire Piccinelli ◆ Redway, California
Pearl Seidman ◆ Concord, California

Project Manager: Micaelia Randolph Brummett

Research Editor: Ann Roper
Graphic Designer: JoAnne Hammer
Production Artists: Normajean Franco and Roy Kutsunai

©1991 Creative Publications
1300 Villa Street
Mountain View, CA 94041
Printed U.S.A.

ISBN: 1-56107-079-3

5 6 7 8 9 10. 9 6 5 4

Table of Contents

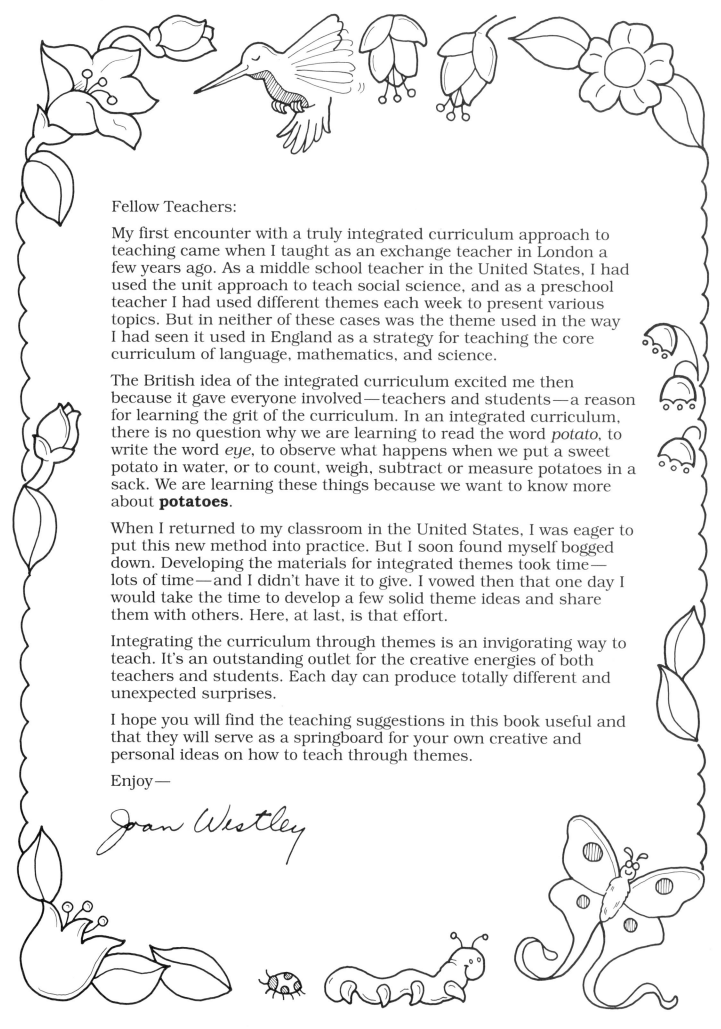

Fellow Teachers:

My first encounter with a truly integrated curriculum approach to teaching came when I taught as an exchange teacher in London a few years ago. As a middle school teacher in the United States, I had used the unit approach to teach social science, and as a preschool teacher I had used different themes each week to present various topics. But in neither of these cases was the theme used in the way I had seen it used in England as a strategy for teaching the core curriculum of language, mathematics, and science.

The British idea of the integrated curriculum excited me then because it gave everyone involved—teachers and students—a reason for learning the grit of the curriculum. In an integrated curriculum, there is no question why we are learning to read the word *potato*, to write the word *eye*, to observe what happens when we put a sweet potato in water, or to count, weigh, subtract or measure potatoes in a sack. We are learning these things because we want to know more about **potatoes**.

When I returned to my classroom in the United States, I was eager to put this new method into practice. But I soon found myself bogged down. Developing the materials for integrated themes took time—lots of time—and I didn't have it to give. I vowed then that one day I would take the time to develop a few solid theme ideas and share them with others. Here, at last, is that effort.

Integrating the curriculum through themes is an invigorating way to teach. It's an outstanding outlet for the creative energies of both teachers and students. Each day can produce totally different and unexpected surprises.

I hope you will find the teaching suggestions in this book useful and that they will serve as a springboard for your own creative and personal ideas on how to teach through themes.

Enjoy—

Joan Westley

THEMEWORKS™ : Houses
©1991 Creative Publications

Teaching Notes

What is *ThemeWorks*™ ?

ThemeWorks is a series of teacher resource books created especially for prekindergarten through grade two teachers who wish to use an integrated approach to teaching the curriculum. Each *ThemeWorks* book centers on one powerful theme. As the children investigate the theme, they engage naturally in language, math, science, cooking, poetry, literature, dramatization and art activities. The theme also provides a springboard for large-scale projects, dramatic play centers, and the construction of classroom environments.

ThemeWorks heavily favors the whole language approach to developing language skills. Children are exposed to language through chants, songs, stories, poems, and rhymes. They are encouraged to play with the rhythmic and repetitive structures in rhymes and chants and they begin the process of writing using these frames. Reading is developed through the children's own speaking and writing.

Counting and number work are developed through meaningful problems that evolve out of real situations relevant to the theme. Emphasis is on number concepts and relationships, organizing numerical data, and measurement.

How were the themes chosen?

There are hundreds of possibilities for themes, but the best themes are those that provide the potential for a broad range of activities across all the curriculum areas. We chose themes that were rich sources for songs, poems, storybooks, and rhymes. Also considered was the theme's appropriateness for the developmental levels and interests of young children. The themes addressed in this first series of 64-page books are:

> Night Time
> Rain
> Houses
> Trees
> At the Seashore
> Under the Ground

How is *ThemeWorks*™ organized?

Each theme is organized into three distinct parts:

- the kickoff,
- the theme activities, and
- the culminating event.

We recommend that each class do the kickoff and the culminating event and then pick the activities they would prefer to do in between. This arrangement allows an individual class to make a theme study as personal as possible and to adjust the length of time devoted to a particular theme to meet individual needs.

What is the kickoff?

We begin each theme with a kickoff event related to the theme. For example, the exploration of the night time theme kicks off with a pretend sleepover at school. This activity gives everyone involved a sense of expectation about the theme that is to be studied.

The kickoff is designed to capitalize on what children already know about the topic rather than require any specialized knowledge or skills. It also provides an informal assessment of what students already know about a topic. It starts them focusing their thinking on what they want to learn about the theme.

The theme mascot is also introduced during the kickoff. This mascot is a puppet character that serves to give instructions, introduce new ideas and songs, and provide friendly guidance throughout the theme study.

This is also a good time to begin a theme web and a word bank.

What is a web?

A web is a brainstorming tool and graphic organizer. At the center of the web is the name of the current theme. As children name subtopics of the theme, each idea is connected to the center by lines. Through this brainstorming process, the class begins to see all the avenues of exploration that are available to them through the vehicle of the theme. Work on the web can go on throughout the investigation of the theme. A sample web is shown on page 8.

What is a word bank?

A word bank is a dictionary of words related to the theme. Entries for the word bank may be suggested by the children any time throughout the exploration of the theme. A sample word bank is shown on page 8.

What happens after the kickoff?

Between the opening and culminating events, each *ThemeWorks* resource book offers 18 mini-topics related to the theme at large. Each mini-topic is presented on a two-page spread. By scanning the Table of Contents, a teacher can choose those topics she feels are most appropriate for her class's study of the theme at hand.

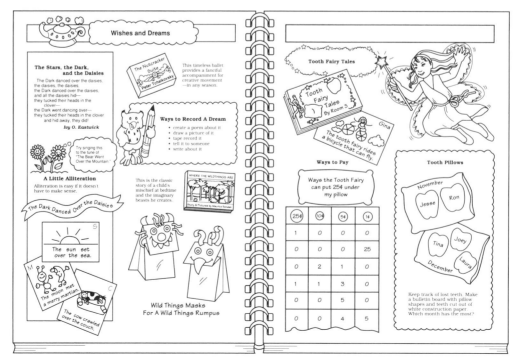

THEMEWORKS™ : Houses
©1991 Creative Publications

How does the theme exploration end?

At the end of each *ThemeWorks* book is a suggestion for a culminating event. In Night Time, for example, the theme study culminates in a pretend campout at school. Each of the events is an outgrowth of many of the theme activities that have gone before. Throughout the theme exploration, children prepare for the culminating event by creating special artwork or construction projects that form the environment of the final event. The culminating event is a good way to end the theme exploration because it gives students a sense of accomplishment, and a chance to show what they know. The children present some of the work they have done, sing the songs they have learned, play some of the games—all within a context relevant to the theme.

Houses

Our exploration of houses takes us from observations of houses to building a house, to looking at houses around the world and long ago, to a study of animal homes, as well as some fun with some favorite children's stories and rhymes that have houses as a theme (*The Three Bears, Hansel and Gretel, The House That Jack Built, The Three Pigs,* and *The Old Woman Who Lived in a Shoe*). We also touch on some emotional aspects of houses: the fears we have about scary things and scary places in houses and the feelings we have about moving away from our homes.

A House Web

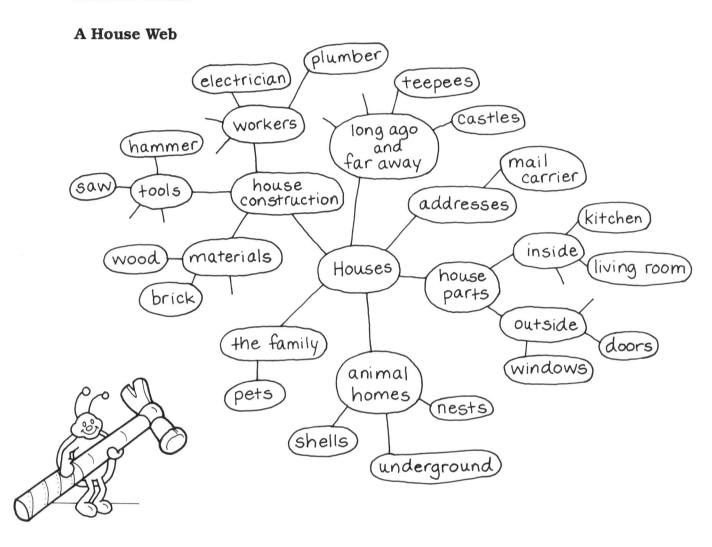

Houses Word Bank

house	chimney	kitchen	playroom
turtle	home	porch	living room
basement	crab	roof	garage
dining room	mailbox	snail	door
driveway	hall	shell	nest
window	yard	bathroom	ant
spider	wall	fence	bedroom
bee	web		

THEMEWORKS™ : Houses
©1991 Creative Publications

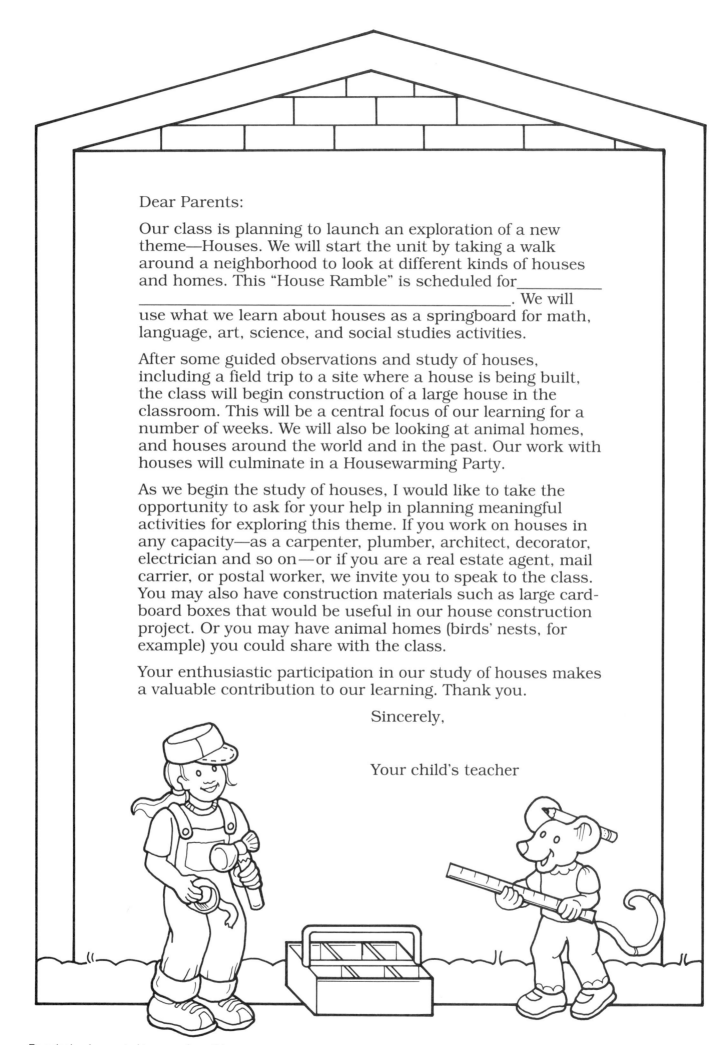

Dear Parents:

Our class is planning to launch an exploration of a new theme—Houses. We will start the unit by taking a walk around a neighborhood to look at different kinds of houses and homes. This "House Ramble" is scheduled for_____ _____. We will use what we learn about houses as a springboard for math, language, art, science, and social studies activities.

After some guided observations and study of houses, including a field trip to a site where a house is being built, the class will begin construction of a large house in the classroom. This will be a central focus of our learning for a number of weeks. We will also be looking at animal homes, and houses around the world and in the past. Our work with houses will culminate in a Housewarming Party.

As we begin the study of houses, I would like to take the opportunity to ask for your help in planning meaningful activities for exploring this theme. If you work on houses in any capacity—as a carpenter, plumber, architect, decorator, electrician and so on—or if you are a real estate agent, mail carrier, or postal worker, we invite you to speak to the class. You may also have construction materials such as large cardboard boxes that would be useful in our house construction project. Or you may have animal homes (birds' nests, for example) you could share with the class.

Your enthusiastic participation in our study of houses makes a valuable contribution to our learning. Thank you.

Sincerely,

Your child's teacher

Our opening event for this theme is a house ramble, a walk around the neighborhood to look at different kinds of houses. Children can be assigned to "clubs,"—different groups that focus on a particular house feature as we walk.

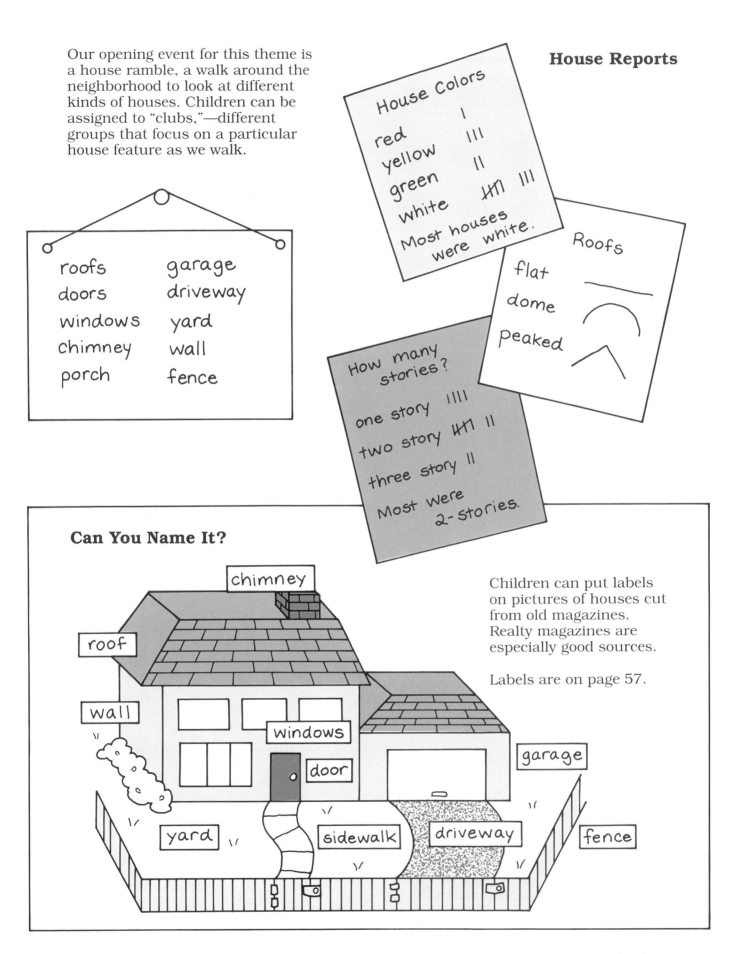

roofs   garage
doors   driveway
windows   yard
chimney   wall
porch   fence

House Reports

House Colors
red I
yellow III
green II
white 卌 III
Most houses were white.

Roofs
flat
dome
peaked

How many stories?
one story IIII
two story 卌 II
three story II
Most were 2-stories.

Can You Name It?

chimney
roof
wall
windows
door
garage
yard
sidewalk
driveway
fence

Children can put labels on pictures of houses cut from old magazines. Realty magazines are especially good sources.

Labels are on page 57.

THEMEWORKS™ : Houses
©1991 Creative Publications

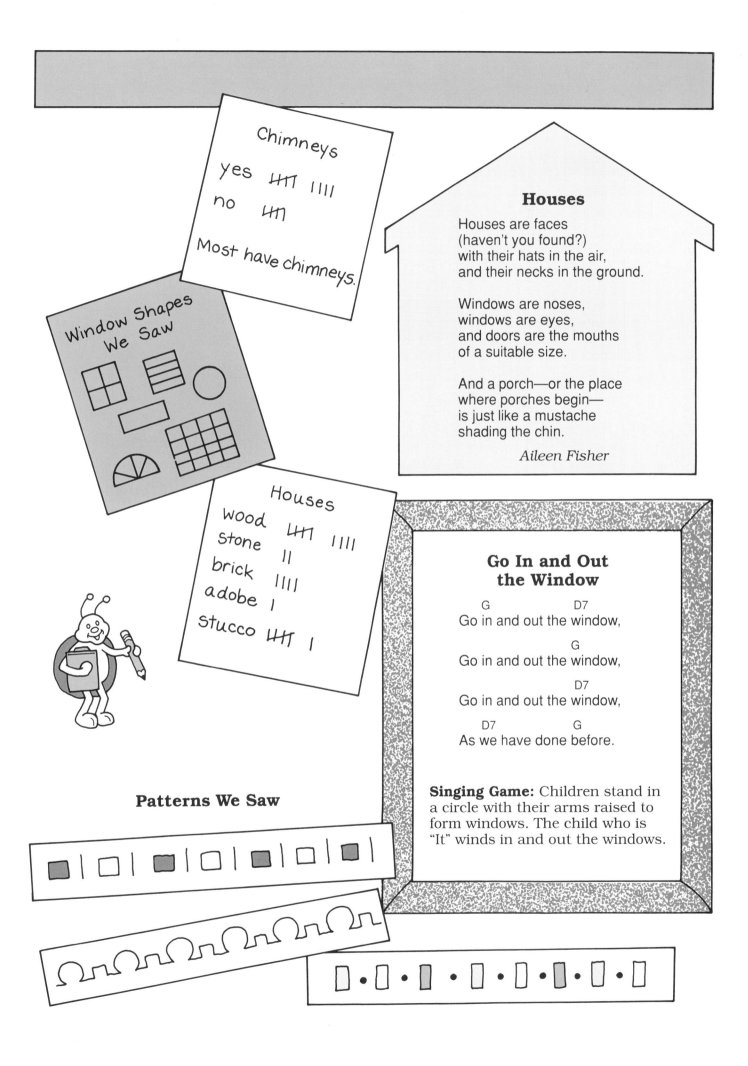

Chimneys

yes ⊬⊬⊬ IIII

no ⊬⊬⊬

Most have chimneys.

Window Shapes
We Saw

Houses

Houses are faces
(haven't you found?)
with their hats in the air,
and their necks in the ground.

Windows are noses,
windows are eyes,
and doors are the mouths
of a suitable size.

And a porch—or the place
where porches begin—
is just like a mustache
shading the chin.

Aileen Fisher

Houses

wood ⊬⊬⊬ IIII

stone II

brick IIII

adobe I

stucco ⊬⊬⊬ I

**Go In and Out
the Window**

G   D7
Go in and out the window,

G
Go in and out the window,

D7
Go in and out the window,

D7   G
As we have done before.

Singing Game: Children stand in
a circle with their arms raised to
form windows. The child who is
"It" winds in and out the windows.

Patterns We Saw

Introducing Molly Mouse

Molly Mouse, our mascot for this theme, is a friendly house mouse. She's a great house explorer, as she is both curious and observant. Her small size makes it easy for her to get around and explore everything around her. She sings and tells stories too.

Molly Mouse puppet:

felt eyes, ears, and nose

fishing line whiskers

gray sock

yarn tail

The Town Mouse and the Country Mouse

In Aesop's fable, the town mouse persuades his country cousin to taste the luxuries of city living but its dangers are also revealed.

Where do you want your house, little mouse?

Michelle

Mouse house for a country mouse.

Sean

Mouse house for a town mouse.

A Game of Cat and Mouse

One child is the cat while the others pretend to be house mice. When the cat turns its back and counts to a number the teacher designates, the mice romp around. When the cat turns around, the mice try to get back to designated mice holes before the cat catches them. A caught mouse becomes the next cat.

OU Words

house	shout	crowd
mouse	about	pow
town	cloud	bow-wow
out	crown	loud

THEMEWORKS™ : Houses
©1991 Creative Publications

Hickory Dickory Dock

Hickory dickory dock
The mouse ran up the clock.
The clock struck one
The mouse ran down.
Hickory dickory dock.

Our made-up verses:

The clock struck two
The mouse felt like new.

The clock struck three
The mouse said "Wheeee."

The clock struck four
The mouse closed the door.

The clock struck five...

Mice

I think mice
Are rather nice.

Their tails are long,
Their faces small,
They haven't any
Chins at all.
Their ears are pink,
Their teeth are white,
They run about
The house at night.
They nibble things
They shouldn't touch
And no one seems
To like them much.

But I think mice
Are nice.

Rose Fyleman

Molly's Walk

After reading *Rosie's Walk* by Pat Hutchins (Macmillan, 1968), the class can create a similar story in which the theme character, Molly Mouse, goes for a walk around the house with a cat lurking nearby.

On the Bookshelf

The adventures of a real house mouse and his not-so-real-friend, the wind-up mouse.

Molly the Mouse went for a walk around the house.

Nita — over the chair

Cliff — behind the stove

Debbie — under the bed

Here is a House
(fingerplay)

Here is a house built up high
  (arms up with fingertips touching to
  form roof)
With two tall chimneys reaching the sky
  (two fingers pointing up)
Here are the windows
  (form windows with fingers)
And here is the door.
  (knock)
If you peek inside, you'll see a mouse
on the floor.
  (raise hands in fright)

Rooms in the House

kitchen	bathroom
living room	bedroom
dining room	playroom
hall	

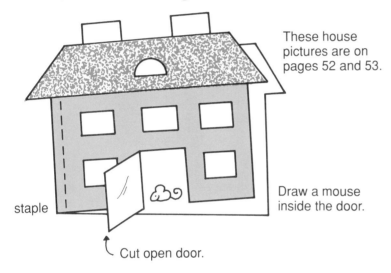

These house pictures are on pages 52 and 53.

Draw a mouse inside the door.

staple

Cut open door.

Open the door and you will see a mouse on the floor!

What do you see when you open the windows?

Shoebox Rooms

Put the boxes together to form a shoebox house.

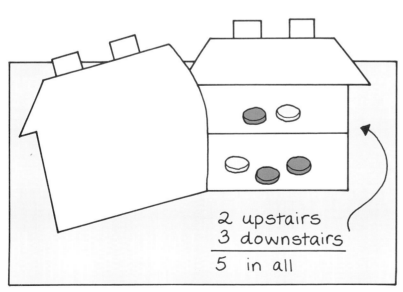

2 upstairs
3 downstairs
─────────
5 in all

In Our House

ANNE ROCKWELL

On the Bookshelf

We visit Bear Family's house and see all the familiar things they do in each room.

THEMEWORKS™ : Houses
©1991 Creative Publications

In the Little House

There was a little yellow house,
And in the little yellow house,
There was a little blue room,
And in the little blue room,
There was a little brown desk,
And in the little brown desk,
There was a little white box,
And in the little white box,
There was a little red heart.

Children can create and illustrate their own variations of this jingle.

On the Bookshelf

This song is the tale of a kindly man who lets every passerby take shelter in his wee house in the heather. When the house falls down from all the people, the visitors build him a larger house.

In the House Number Book

Our Number Book Room 52

Jamie — 1 stove

Dennis — 2 fireplaces

Aaron — 3 tables

Sheri — 4 beds

Lee — 5 chairs

Kaoru — 6 steps

Elaine — 7 lightbulbs

Roy — 8 plates

Fernando — 9 doors

Calvin — 10 windows

Home is a Special Place

HOME
SWEET
HOME

Our House

Our house is small—
The lawn and all
Can scarcely hold the flowers,
Yet every bit,
The whole of it,
Is precious, for it's ours!

From door to door,
From roof to floor,
From wall to wall we love it;
We wouldn't change
For something strange
One shabby corner of it!

The space complete
In cubic feet
From cellar floor to rafter
Just measures right,
And not too tight,
For us, and friends, and laughter!

Dorothy Brown Thompson

This Is My House

Children carefully observe their houses and then draw realistic pictures of them being careful to include the correct number of windows, doors in the proper places and using the correct colors.

On the Bookshelf

A boy tells why his house is special.

MY HOUSE
Story: MIRIAM SCHLEIN
Pictures: JOE LASKER

House Graph

apartment house

duplex

one-family

What other ways can we graph our house pictures?

THEMEWORKS™ : Houses
©1991 Creative Publications

Sights and Sounds

I see _____,
I see _____,
I see _____,
In my house.

I hear _____,
I hear _____,
I hear _____,
In my house.

Home! You're Where It's Warm Inside

Home! You are a special place;
you're where I wake and wash my face,
brush my teeth and comb my hair,
change my socks and underwear,
clean my ears and blow my nose,
try on all my parents' clothes.

Home! You're where it's warm inside,
where my tears are gently dried,
where I'm comforted and fed,
where I'm forced to go to bed,
where there's always love to spare;
Home! I'm glad that you are there.

Jack Prelutsky

House Surveys

My house has
____ doors
____ windows
____ rooms
____ chimneys
____ steps

My house has
1 _____
2 _____
3 _____
4 _____
5 _____

Numbers in My House

1:05

810

Shapes in My House

Colors in My House

blue curtains

brown chair

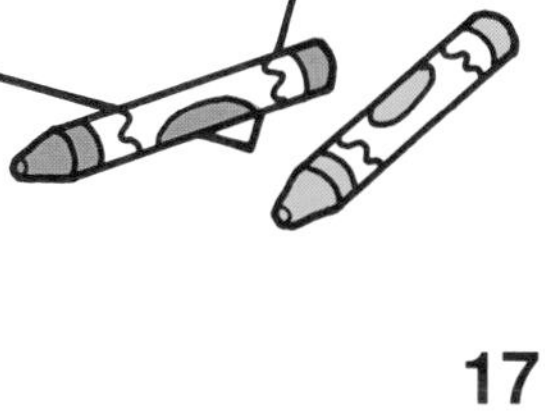

 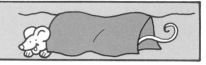

A Secret House All My Own

Children like to create their own secret places—whether it be an elaborate tree house, or just a special corner of a room.

On the Bookshelf

Evan longs for privacy and a place of his own.

Sally creates a secret home in the garden.

Everyone should have a little house of their own—under an umbrella, in a cardboard box, or up in a tree house.

A child imagines a house where you can jump on beds, swing on doors, and write on walls.

My Secret House

I have a secret house.
It has _____ _____.
It has _____ _____.
It has _____ _____.
I like my secret house.

In my secret house,
I can _____.
I can _____.
I can _____.
I like my secret house.

Tree House

Sara
We climb a rope up to our house.

Matthew
We play pirates in our house.

Katie
We drank lemonade in our house.

Jose
I like my treehouse.

Zooey
The treehouse is my secret place.

THEMEWORKS™ : Houses
©1991 Creative Publications

Invitations

Dear Amy,

Please come to my secret house for lunch. Come on Saturday at 12:00.

Your friend,
Leah

On the Bookshelf

Geometric shapes tell this story.

There Was a Crooked Man

A
There was a crooked man

E
And he walked a crooked mile,

A
He found a crooked sixpence

E
Upon a crooked stile.

A
He bought a crooked cat

D
Which caught a crooked mouse

E
And they all lived together

A
In a little crooked house.

It's fun to assume crooked postures while we sing this song.

Odd-Shaped Houses

Geometric shapes cut from colored paper.

Gina
The triangle man in his
Triangle House.

Pablo
The square man in his
Square House.

Jonathan
The round man in his
Round House.

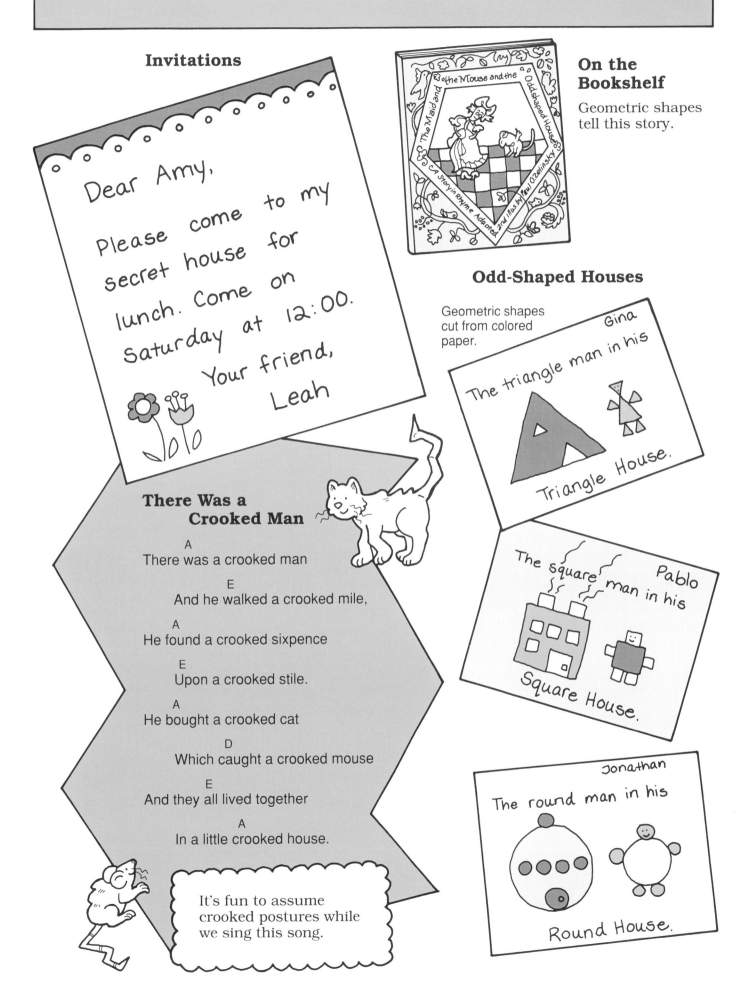

Monsters in the House

On the Bookshelf

Children's fears are often focused on certain places in the house—in the basement, the attic, a closet, or under a stairwell. The following books deal with these fears.

A boy confronts a monster in his closet and learns it is not so scary after all.

A boy out-smarts the alligator under his bed by setting a trap for him.

Harry is afraid when his mother goes down to the cellar and does not return right away.

Our Book of Fears

Sarah — There's a witch under the steps.

Keith — There's a two-headed dog in the attic.

Scary Things, Scary Places

Scary Things	Scary Places
monster	in the closet
ghost	under the dresser
dragon	in the basement
wolf	under the steps

The Dark House

In a dark, dark wood, there was a dark, dark house,
And in that dark, dark house, there was a dark, dark room,
And in that dark, dark room, there was a dark, dark cupboard,
And in that dark, dark cupboard, there was a dark, dark shelf,
And on that dark, dark shelf, there was a dark, dark box,
And in that dark, dark box...
There was a GHOST!

The children can chant each line with GHOSTLY voices!

What variations of this chant can the class create?

THEMEWORKS™ : Houses
©1991 Creative Publications

The Scariest Place in the House

basement					
closet					
attic					

Are You Afraid of Ghosts?

yes	✓	✓	✓	✓	✓	✓	
no	✓	✓	✓	✓			

A Goblin Lives in Our House

A goblin lives in our house,
in our house, in our house,
A goblin lives in our house
all the year round.
He bumps
And he jumps
And he thumps
And he stumps
He knocks
And he rocks
And he rattles at the locks.
A goblin lives in our house,
in our house, in our house,
A goblin lives in our house
all the year round.

Rose Fyleman

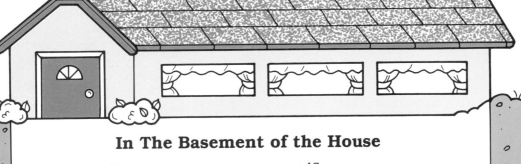

In The Basement of the House

       D   A7
There's a _____ in the basement of the house.

     A7   D
There's a _____ in the basement of the house.

     G
There's a _____ , there's a _____ ,

     D
There's a _____ , there's a _____ .

   A7   D
There's a _____ in the basement of the house.

There's a _____ in the _____ in the basement of the house.
There's a _____ in the _____ in the basement of the house.
There's a _____ , there's a _____ ,
There's a _____ , there's a _____ .
There's a _____ in the basement of the house.

There's a _____ in the _____ in the _____ in the basement
    of the house...

As this poem is read, the children clap on the word *our* and pantomime these actions:

    bumps
    jumps
    thumps
    stumps
    knocks
    rocks
    rattles at the locks

Oh, Do You Know?

The old favorite *The Muffin Man* can be individualized to give children practice remembering their street names.

F
Oh, do you know (children's name),

B♭   C7
(children's name), (children's name)?

F
Oh, do you know (children's name),

C7
Who lives on (street name).

Oh, yes I know (children's name)...

A Postcard to Myself

Jake McDonald
210 Abernathy
Madison, WI
22201

Parents can help children write their addresses on one side of a 4" x 6" card. Then the children can draw a picture on the other side.

Children get a thrill out of receiving their own postcards. It doesn't seem to matter that they sent them to themselves.

Make an outing of buying the stamps at the post office and mailing the postcards in a mailbox.

On the Bookshelf

THE POST OFFICE BOOK
Mail and How It Moves
by Gail Gibbons

THE JOLLY POSTMAN
or Other People's Letters
JANET & ALLAN AHLBERG

Class Visitor

The neighborhood mail carrier could be asked to visit the class to explain what he or she does and to answer the children's questions.

U.S. MAIL

THEMEWORKS™ : Houses
©1991 Creative Publications

Dramatic Play: Mail Carrier

Dress Up Clothes

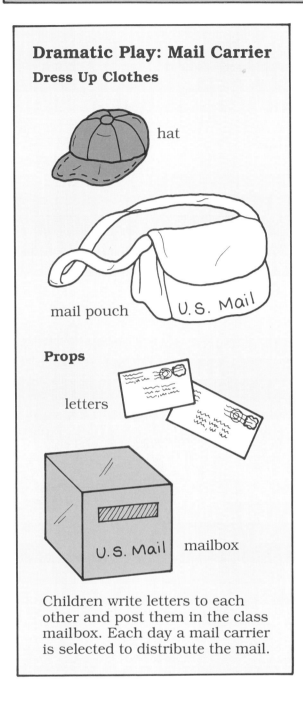

hat

mail pouch

U.S. Mail

Props

letters

U.S. Mail mailbox

Children write letters to each other and post them in the class mailbox. Each day a mail carrier is selected to distribute the mail.

A Tisket, A Tasket

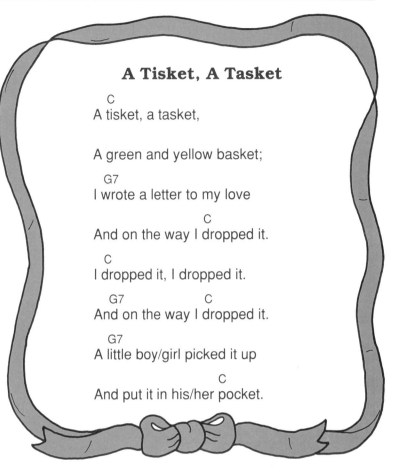

C
A tisket, a tasket,

A green and yellow basket;

G7
I wrote a letter to my love

C
And on the way I dropped it.

C
I dropped it, I dropped it.

G7   C
And on the way I dropped it.

G7
A little boy/girl picked it up

C
And put it in his/her pocket.

The children form a circle. The child who is "It" skips around the outside of the circle and drops a letter (traditionally a handkerchief) behind a child in the circle as the song is sung. This child picks up the letter and tries to beat "It" back to the vacated space in the circle.

Put Your Houses In Order

Children take turns switching pairs of houses until all the house numbers are in order.

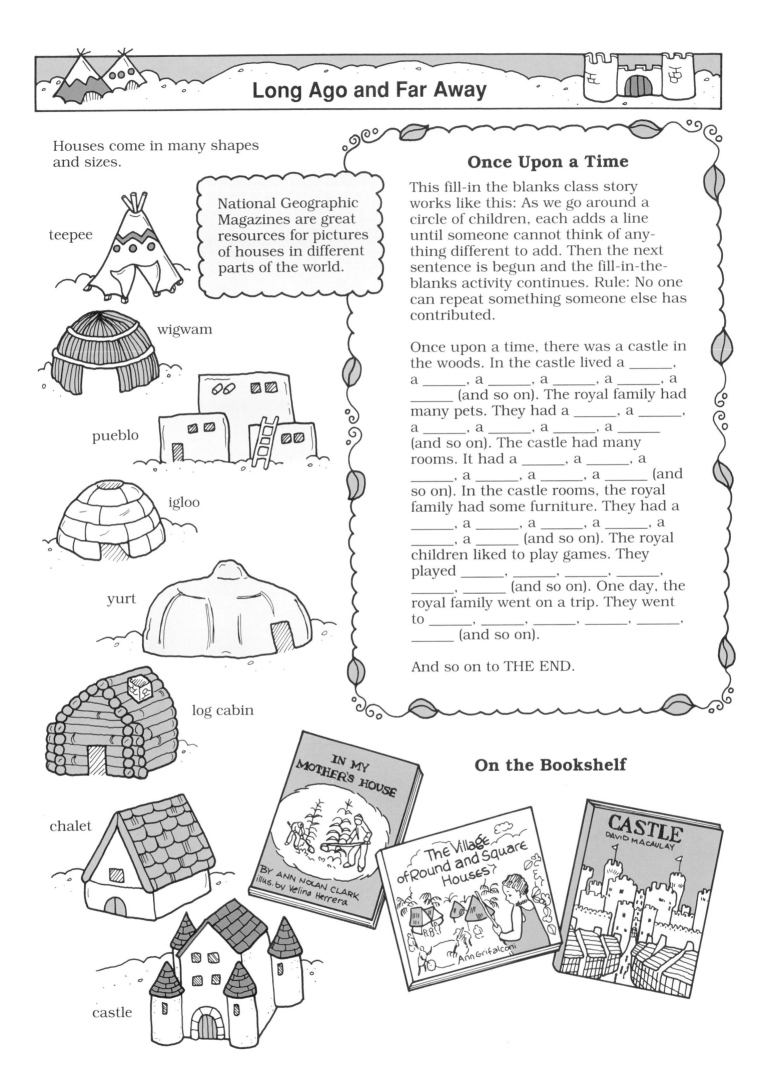

Houses come in many shapes and sizes.

teepee

National Geographic Magazines are great resources for pictures of houses in different parts of the world.

wigwam

pueblo

igloo

yurt

log cabin

chalet

castle

Once Upon a Time

This fill-in the blanks class story works like this: As we go around a circle of children, each adds a line until someone cannot think of anything different to add. Then the next sentence is begun and the fill-in-the-blanks activity continues. Rule: No one can repeat something someone else has contributed.

Once upon a time, there was a castle in the woods. In the castle lived a _____, a _____, a _____, a _____, a _____, a _____ (and so on). The royal family had many pets. They had a _____, a _____, a _____, a _____, a _____, a _____ (and so on). The castle had many rooms. It had a _____, a _____, a _____, a _____, a _____, a _____ (and so on). In the castle rooms, the royal family had some furniture. They had a _____, a _____, a _____, a _____, a _____, a _____ (and so on). The royal children liked to play games. They played _____, _____, _____, _____, _____, _____ (and so on). One day, the royal family went on a trip. They went to _____, _____, _____, _____, _____, _____ (and so on).

And so on to THE END.

On the Bookshelf

IN MY MOTHER'S HOUSE
BY ANN NOLAN CLARK
illus. by Velina Herrera

The Village of Round and Square Houses
Ann Grifalconi

CASTLE
DAVID MACAULAY

THEMEWORKS™ : Houses
©1991 Creative Publications

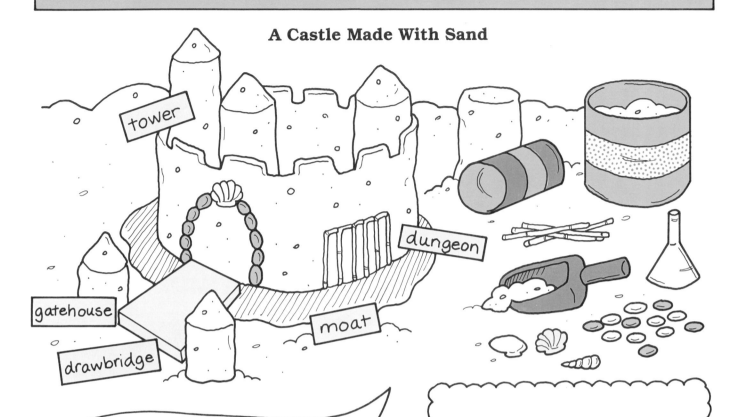

A Castle Made With Sand

tower

gatehouse

drawbridge

dungeon

moat

Sing a Song of Sixpence

C
Sing a song of sixpence

G7
A pocket full of rye,

G7
Four and twenty blackbirds

C
Baked in a pie;

C
When the pie was opened,

G7
The birds began to sing,

G7
Wasn't that a dainty dish

C
To set before the king?

The king was in the counting house,
Counting out his money,
The queen was in the parlor,
Eating bread and honey,
The maid was in the garden,
Hanging out the clothes,
When along came a blackbird
And kissed her pretty nose.

What fairy tales take place in castles?
Snow White
Sleeping Beauty
Cinderella

Which fairy tales do not take place in castles?
Three Bears

Castles

Bricks stacked up
from a
torn down building
make
a castle
thick and strong.

Empty cans
can do
for towers
if you stack them
low
and long.

Marci Ridlon

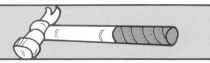
A Visit to a Construction Site

If a house is being constructed close by, you will not want to miss the opportunity for students to see what it takes to build a house from the ground up. They can interview the construction workers on the job and observe what each professional contributes. Revisiting the site periodically will give students perspective on this complicated undertaking.

A few words of warning are in order. First, it is best to plan and organize the trip carefully. Second, the visit should be arranged well in advance with the contractor. And third, the children should be warned that in no case should they ever visit a construction site on their own.

Reference Books

Photo Exhibit

Photos can be taken at a construction site.

A big hole was dug.

A foundation was poured.

The walls went up.

The roof went on.

The house was painted.

The children put the photographs in order and dictate captions for each.

THEMEWORKS™ : Houses
©1991 Creative Publications

Model Houses

Each child makes a small house, which can be made part of a village (see below). To control the size of the houses children make so they will fit on a common terrain, you can give each child a "plot," a piece of cardboard the size you want them to work with.

Ideas for House Materials

wood scraps	rocks
cardboard boxes	clay
Lincoln Logs	adobe bricks (see below)
Legos®	
notched popsicle® sticks	
styrofoam® blocks	

Shapes (circles, squares, rectangles) cut from construction paper can be used for doors and windows.

The Terrain

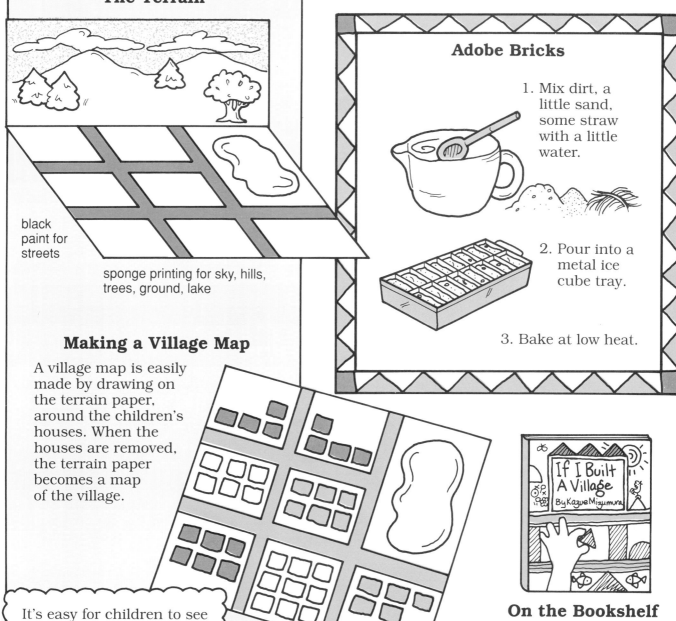

black paint for streets

sponge printing for sky, hills, trees, ground, lake

Adobe Bricks

1. Mix dirt, a little sand, some straw with a little water.

2. Pour into a metal ice cube tray.

3. Bake at low heat.

Making a Village Map

A village map is easily made by drawing on the terrain paper, around the children's houses. When the houses are removed, the terrain paper becomes a map of the village.

It's easy for children to see the connection between the two-dimensional map and the three-dimensional village it represents.

Village Map

On the Bookshelf

A poem about a child who builds a village out of blocks.

If I Built A Village By Kazue Mizumura

Dramatic Play:
The Hardware Store

Dress-Up Clothes
   clerk smocks
   caps

Props
   merchandise
   wood
   tools
   cash register
   price tags
   play money

Roles
   clerks
   customers

A visit to a nearby hardware store or lumber yard will make the role playing all the more interesting and real for the children.

Comparison Shopping: Tools

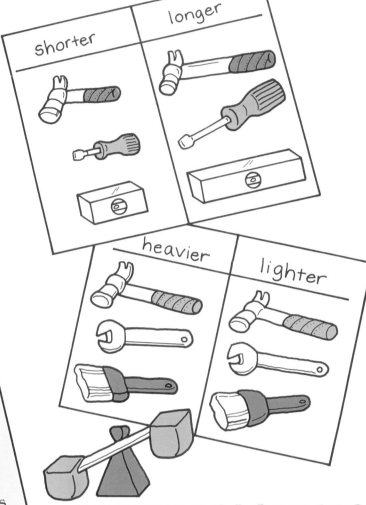

Dear Parents:

In our current study of houses, we are focusing on people who help build houses. If you are a construction worker, we would like to interview you. Please be our guest one day. Bring the tools of your trade, wear your work uniform (if you have one), and be ready for lots of questions.

Thank you,
Room 6

Mike's Mom

Dear Ms. Nist,

Thank you for visiting our class. Now we know what plumbers do.

Room 6

On the Bookshelf

Once There Was a House and you can make it!
Devised by Gregg Reyes
Written by Judy Hindley
illus. by Robert Bartelt
A make and play PICTUREBACK

Neighborhood friends make houses for themselves out of cardboard boxes.

Detailed instructions show how to make child-size cardboard box houses with real doors, windows, gutters, doorknobs, locks, chimneys, antennae, mail slot.

THEMEWORKS™ : Houses
©1991 Creative Publications

Foundation Experiments

Each group of children gets a tall, narrow block of wood to use as a tower. The challenge: to find a way to make the tower stand up so that it cannot be blown over in a strong wind.

The House That We Built

This is the house that _____ built.

This is the _____
that lay in the house that _____ built.

This is the _____
that _____ the _____
that lay in the house that _____ built.

This is the _____
that _____ the _____
that _____ the _____
that lay in the house that _____ built.

This is the _____
that _____ the _____
that _____ the _____
that _____ the _____
that lay in the house that _____ built.

And so on.

O Our Experiment   Eileen
                    Lisa

We tried to make the tower strong. We tried many

O ways. The best way was to set it deep in a box of sand. Then it was very strong. We could not blow

O it down.

On the Bookshelf

The library has many, many versions of *The House That Jack Built*. Here's a rebus version. Look for Antonio Frasconi's version in two languages.

Also see page 54.

This is the house that We built.

This is the cheese that lay in the house that we built.

This is the mouse that ate the cheese that lay in the house that We built.

This is the cat that scared the mouse that ate the cheese that lay in the house that we built.

This is the dog that chased the cat that scared the mouse that ate the cheese that lay in the house that we built.

Dramatic Play: Construction Site

The block corner is a good location for this dramatic play activity. The activity can evolve from play with pretend buildings to the construction of an actual "big house" in the classroom.

Dress Up Clothes
work gloves
hard hats (see description)
overalls
work boots
safety goggles
tool belt

Props

Tools:
hammer
screwdrivers
clamps
wrench
place
ruler
file
paintbrushes
paint rollers
paint trays
paint buckets
level
plumb bob

These props can be handled safely by children when they are told how to use them.

Equipment:
sandpaper
wallpaper
nails
blueprint
pipe
wire
lunch pails
crane (see description)

Roles
architect
contractor
surveyor
carpenter
electrician
plumber
painter
bricklayer
inspector
roofer

How to Make a Hard Hat

papier-mâché

balloon

Break the balloon when the papier-mâché dries. Then paint the hard hat.

How to Make a Crane

long box

large box with holes cut as shown

dowel held by child crane operator

hook

large box with hole for other box

This rope threads through the long box and winds around dowel.

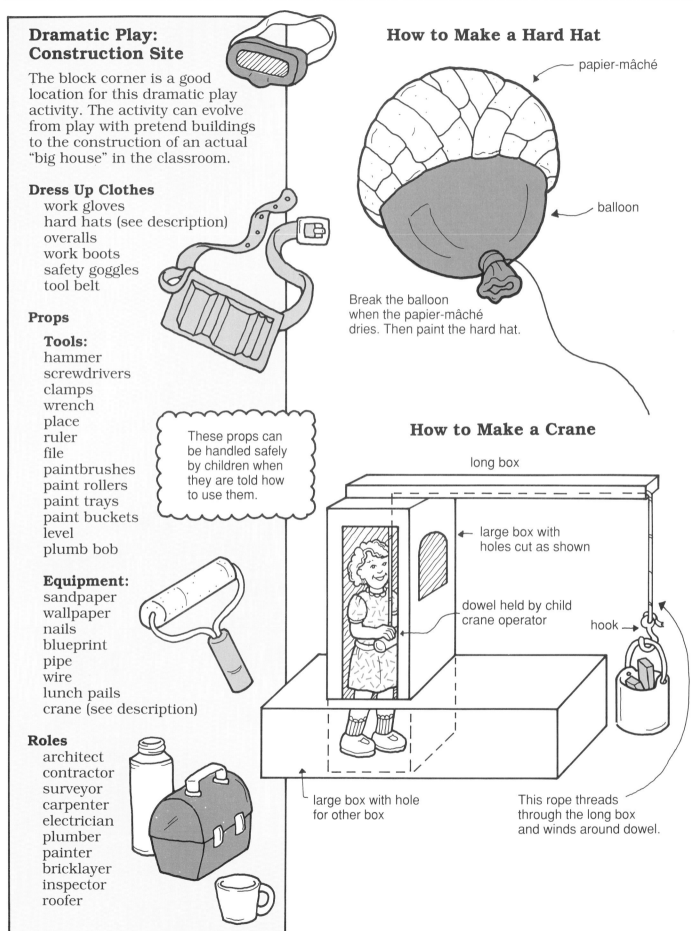

THEMEWORKS™ : Houses
©1991 Creative Publications

A Worker's Lunch

Egg Salad Sandwiches

1. Boil an egg.

   15 minutes 🕐 🕐

2. Cool the egg.

3. Peel the egg.

4. Chop the egg.

5. Add mayonnaise.

   CREAMY MAYONNAISE

6. Make a sandwich.

The Big House

In the classroom, children create a large house made out of boxes and cardboard. When the Big House is finished, we celebrate with an Open House (see pages 48 to 51).

On the Bookshelf

Each family member wants to paint the house a different color.

THE HOUSE OF FOUR SEASONS
by Roger Duvoisin

Kindergarten Construction Company

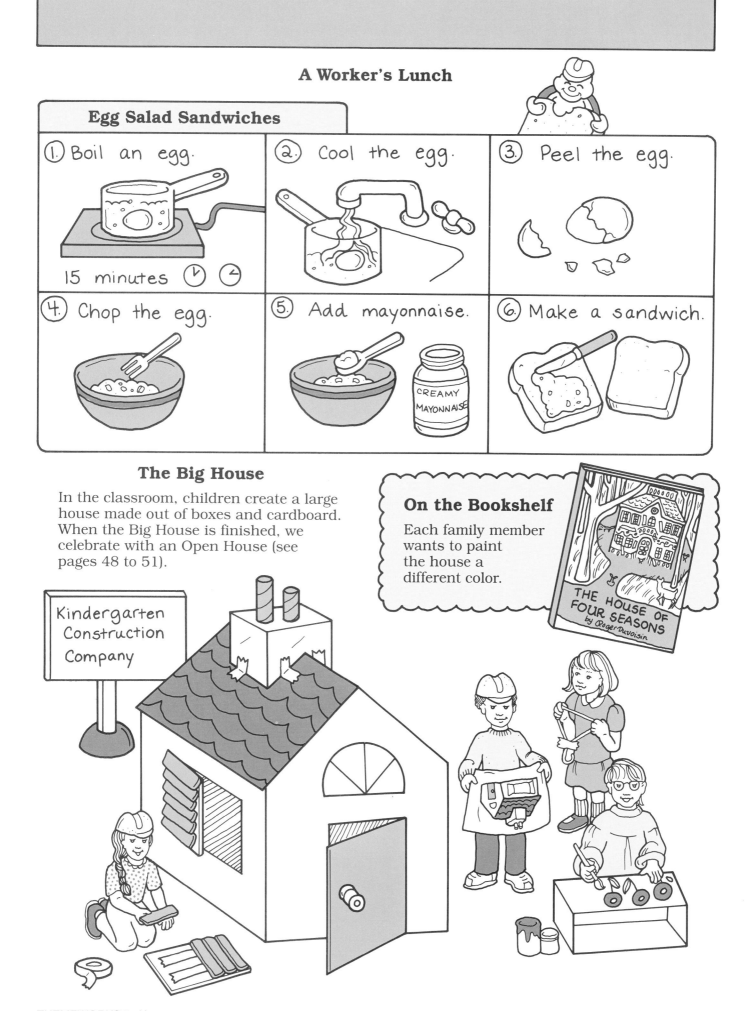

Dramatic Play: The Family

Use the Big House (see page 31) for the setting of this dramatic play.

Dress Up Clothes
aprons
purses
hats
vests
jewelry
high-heeled shoes
jackets
ties
nightgowns
robe
bridal clothing

Props
eyeglass frames
wigs
shawls
newspapers
canes
baby blankets
baby dolls
iron
dishes
duster
mop
bucket

Furniture
cradle or crib
rocking chair
stroller
sink
stove
refrigerator

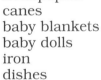

Family Tree

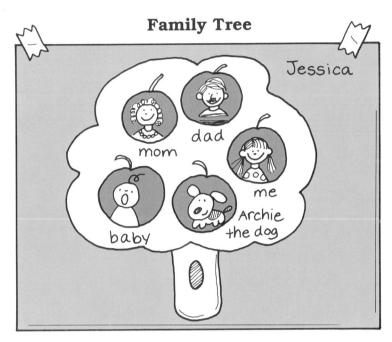

Jessica

mom
dad
me
baby
Archie the dog

Mother May I?

The children stand in a row. One child, the "mother," calls out the names of the players in turn and gives directions such as "Sharon, take two giant steps." The child asks "Mother, may I?" before following the directions. A child who fails to say "Mother, may I?," loses the turn. The first child to reach "mother" becomes the "mother" for the next round.

Mother, may I?

On the Bookshelf

MY MOTHER'S HOUSE, MY FATHER'S HOUSE

by C.B. Christiansen illus. by Irene Trivas

A child travels back and forth between her two parents' houses.

Do You Have a Sister?

Make another graph for brothers.

yes	X	X	X	X	X	X	X
no	X	X	X	X			

THEMEWORKS™ : Houses
©1991 Creative Publications

Pet Portraits

Luisa

This is Willie the cat.

Roger

This is Hamlet, our dog.

Pet Show

It is best to have house pets visit the class only briefly (no more than half an hour) and only one at a time.

Some questions to ask a pet owner:

- How much does your pet weigh?
- How old is it?
- What does it like to eat?
- Where does it sleep?
- How do you groom your pet?
- What other things do you do to take care of your pet?
- Have you ever taken your pet to the vet?
- For what reason?

Mother Doesn't Want a Dog

Mother doesn't want a dog.
Mother says they smell,
And never sit when you say sit,
Or even when you yell.
And when you come home late at night
And there is ice and snow,
You have to go back out because
The dumb dog has to go.

Mother doesn't want a dog.
Mother says they shed,
And always let the strangers in
And bark at friends instead,
And do disgraceful things on rugs,
And track mud on the floor,
And flop upon your bed at night
And snore their doggy snore.

Mother doesn't want a dog.
She's making a mistake.
Because, more than a dog, I think
She will not want this snake.

Judith Viorst

Pet Awards

The class votes on the friendliest, smallest, strangest, and biggest pets in the classroom. They are likely to think of other categories too!

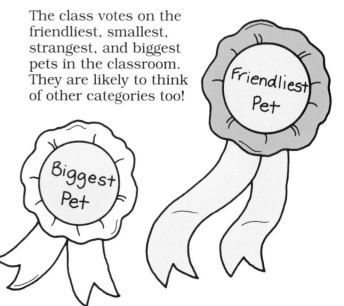

Strangest Pet

Smallest Pet

Biggest Pet

Friendliest Pet

On the Bookshelf

How are the stories different?

Which version do you like best? Why?

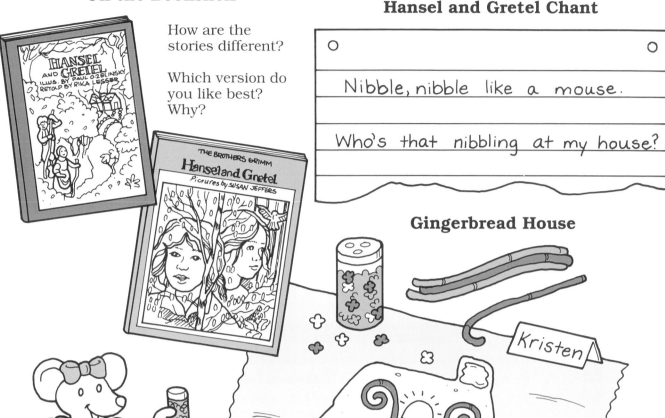

Hansel and Gretel Chant

Nibble, nibble like a mouse.

Who's that nibbling at my house?

Gingerbread House

Kristen

waxed paper

ginger cookies cut in house shapes

icings and cake decorations

Rosemary's Ginger Cutout Cookies

1 cup molasses
½ cup shortening
3 cups sifted flour
2 to 3 teaspoons ginger

½ teaspoon soda
1 teaspoon cinnamon
½ teaspoon salt

powdered sugar   vanilla

Heat molasses and pour over shortening; stir until melted. Add sifted dry ingredients. Chill overnight. Roll very thin on floured surface; cut out. Bake on lightly greased cookie sheets for about 10 minutes at 375 degrees.

Decorate with colored icings made with powdered sugar, water, and a bit of vanilla.

Tell About It

What shapes did you use?

What colors did you use?

How many windows does your gingerbread house have?

THEMEWORKS™ : Houses
©1991 Creative Publications

On the Bookshelf

How do these versions compare?

Wolf and Pig Voices

Little pig, little pig, let me come in.

Not by the hair of my chinny-chin-chin.

Then I'll huff and I'll puff

And I'll blow your house in.

One group reads the wolf's lines in deep, strong voices; another group reads the pigs' lines in high-pitched squeaky voices.

Straw, Stick, or Brick?

straw

stick

Estimate: How many bricks in the house?

Which house is strongest?

brick

Three Pigs Finger Puppets

wrap around and tape

We made a straw house, a stick house, and a brick house. Then we tried to blow them down. The straw house was easiest to blow down. We could not blow down the brick house.

The Old Woman Who Lived in a Shoe

There was an old woman
Who lived in a shoe.
She had so many children
She didn't know what to do.
She gave them some broth
Without any bread.
She spanked them all soundly
And sent them to bed.

Mother Goose

So Many Children: What to Do?

What ways can we sort the pipecleaner children?

girls or boys
hair color
eye color
shoes or no shoes
clothing

Shoe House

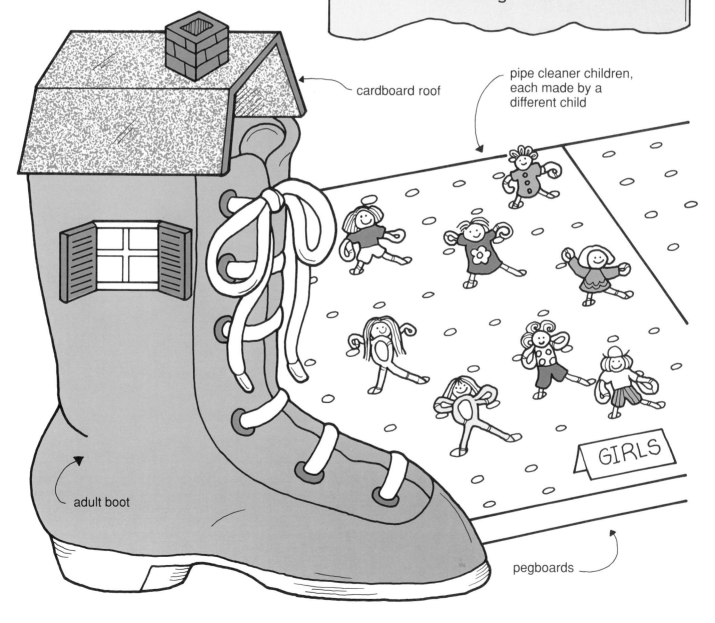

cardboard roof

pipe cleaner children, each made by a different child

adult boot

GIRLS

pegboards

THEMEWORKS™ : Houses
©1991 Creative Publications

How Many Children?

How many children are in your family?

1	●	●	●	●	●	●	●	●		
2	●	●	●	●	●	●	●	●	●	●
3	●	●	●	●						
4	●									
5	●	●	●							
6										
7	●									

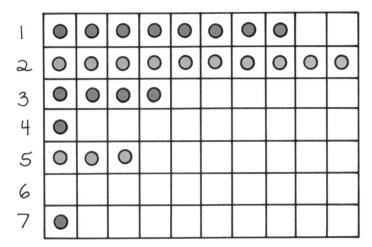

BOYS

The Old Woman

You know the old woman
Who lived in a shoe?
And had so many children
She didn't know what to do?

I think if she lived in
A little shoe-house—
That little old woman was
Surely a mouse!

Beatrix Potter

On the Bookshelf

A family of mice who live in a shoe decide to redecorate.

Rodney Peppé

THE MICE WHO LIVED IN A SHOE

Broth

Cut vegetables into small pieces and cook them in a large pot of water until they are completely soft. Liquify in a blender. Add water to thin, if necessary. Serve warm.

We used
2 potatoes
3 carrots
2 celery stalks
1 onion
5 mushrooms

A Family Story

The classic story of an intruder (Goldilocks) into the happy home of a family of bears should be included in any study of the family and home. Its familiarity and repetitive structure make it a story that can evolve into the children's first experience with theater.

Prop Managers

The prop managers can be responsible for putting the props in order of size for the play production.

The Little Theater

Story
Goldilocks and
The Three Bears

Roles
Papa Bear
Mama Bear
Baby Bear
Goldilocks

Props
small, medium, and
large bowls
small, medium, and
large chairs
small, medium, and
large beds (Use blankets
or rugs.)

HONEY

Three Bear Porridge

OATS

1. rolled oats — 3 T.
2. sunflower seeds — 1 T.
3. raisins — 1 T.
4. apple, chopped — 1 T.
5. powdered milk — 1 T.
6. hot water — ½ c. stir in
7. cover — Turn down when bubbles. Simmer for 15 min.
8. Stir in 8½ t. honey. Eat while warm — when "just right" like Baby Bear's.

just right / too cold / too hot

From *Cook and Learn* by Bev Veitch and Thelma Harms

The Dialogue

The repetitive dialogue in *The Three Bears* can be read from a pocket chart.

Somebody has been | eating | my

sitting in | sleeping in

WHO'S BEEN EATING MY PORRIDGE?

Children enjoy using a deep, low voice for Papa Bear, a medium voice for Mama Bear, and a high, soft, babylike voice for Baby Bear.

On the Bookshelf

Deep in the Forest by BRINTON TURKLE

This wordless book is an exact reversal of the traditional tale. A bear cub takes the place of Goldilocks, and a human family takes the place of the Three Bears. It makes a wonderful comparison with the original story.

Words for a Wordless Book

Children can record the story of *Deep in the Forest* in their own words.

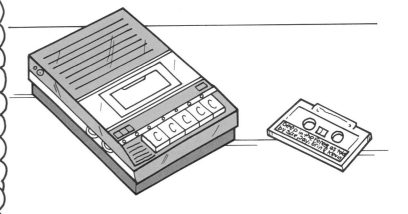

Animal Clubs

The children can work in clubs to investigate an animal and where it lives. Drawing a picture of the animal and its home for a class book can be the culminating club project.

Bears live in caves.

Beavers live in lodges.

Birds live in nests.

Bees live in hives.

Foxes live in dens.

THEMEWORKS™ : Houses
©1991 Creative Publications

Heigh-Ho, Merry-O

Sing verses to the tune of
The Farmer in the Dell.

G
Snails live in shells,

G
Snails live in shells,

G
Heigh-ho, merry-O,

D   G
Snails live in shells.

Foxes live in dens...

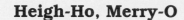

Who Goes There?

The children take turns pantomiming an animal going home (a bird flying to its nest, a rabbit hopping to its warren, an ant creeping to its anthill, and so on). The others guess what animal is being portrayed.

Animal Homes Concentration

Children match animals with their homes. Cards are on page 55-56.

The Very Nicest Place

The fish lives in the brook,
The bird lives in the tree,
But home's the very nicest place
For a little child like me.

Anonymous

The children can create variations, using this poem as a frame.

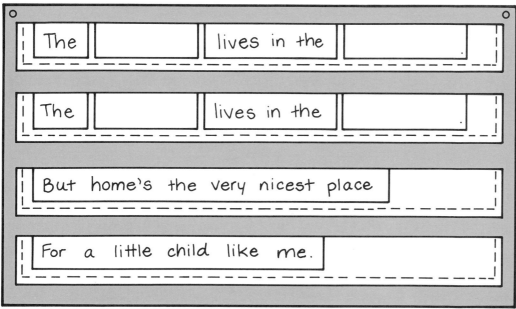

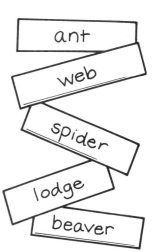

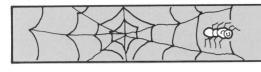 

I Spy an Animal House

Many animal homes can be found on a nature walk in a nearby park. Taking along a pair of "binoculars" helps keep us focused on our search.

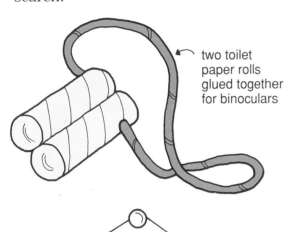

two toilet paper rolls glued together for binoculars

What We Saw

anthills   ⊔⊓⊓

bird's nests ||

gopher's holes   ⊔⊓⊓ ||

spider's webs ||||

The House of the Mouse

The house of the mouse
is a wee little house,
a green little house in the grass,
which big clumsy folk
may hunt and may poke
and still never see as they pass
this sweet little, neat little,
wee little, green little,
cuddle-down hide-away
house in the grass.

Lucy Sprague Mitchell

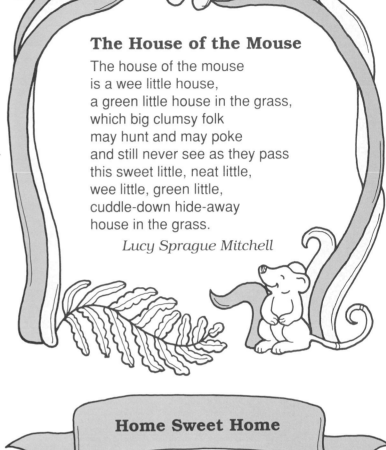

Home Sweet Home

Making a home for an adopted class pet brought in from the wild, requires children to think about what the animal's needs are. What foods does it eat? Does it prefer a wet or a dry environment? Does it like to climb? To dig?

On the Bookshelf

A poem about a little girl's search for animal homes is accompanied by closeup illustrations of the nesting places of familiar animals.

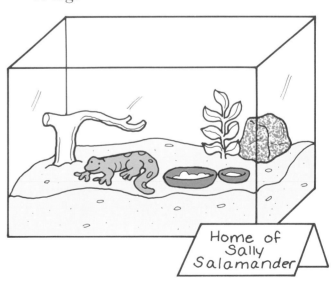

Home of Sally Salamander

THEMEWORKS™ : Houses
©1991 Creative Publications

Birds' Nests

Make sure any nests you remove from the wild are abandoned. Since nests are built in so many different ways, there is an advantage in providing at least two kinds of nests for comparison.

- What kinds of materials were used to make the nest?
- How well does the nest hold together?
- What shape is the nest? How do the nests differ in size, shape, and materials?

Honeycombs

Honeycombs can be bought at health food stores. The comb is built by honeybees out of wax which is secreted from their bodies. In the cells of the honeycomb, nectar collected from flowers is deposited, and eggs are laid.

- How does the beeswax feel? Smell? Taste?
- What shape are the cells?
- How many sides do the cells have?
- Are the cells all the same size?

Ant Colonies

Commercial ant farms provide hours of nature watching, right in the classroom.

- What are the ants doing? Are different ants doing different things?
- Can you find the queen ant?
- How do the ants build their tunnels?
- How many tunnels do you see? Are they connected?
- Are there rooms or chambers in the tunnels? How many can you count? Which is the largest?

Wasp Nests

Wasps make their paper nests with chewed up bits of wood pulp. They usually vacate the nests in the fall.

- What shape is the nest?
- How are the layers of the nest like paper? Does it tear like paper?
- Are there any cells inside the nest? What shape are the cells? How many sides do they have?

Baker's Dough

1 cup flour
¼ cup salt
⅓ cup water

Mix flour and salt. Add water. Form shapes on foil. Bake at a high temperature until the dough is completely hard, but not brown. The amount of time depends upon how thick the dough is.

Baker's Dough Snails

① Roll into long ropes.

② Wind into a spiral.

③ Add antennae.

④ Bake.

⑤ Paint.

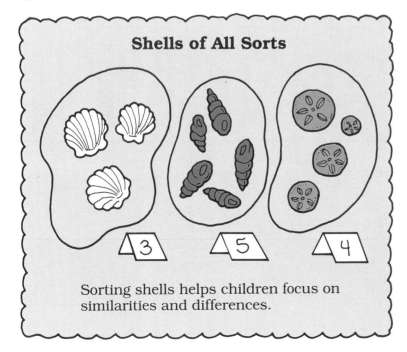

Shells of All Sorts

▷ 3

▱ 5

▷ 4

Sorting shells helps children focus on similarities and differences.

Which snails are bigger than yours? Which are smaller?

Can you put the snails in order of size?

THEMEWORKS™ : Houses
©1991 Creative Publications

Up Close

Snails and hermit crabs are fascinating creatures for children to observe. Both snails and hermit tree crabs are sometimes available in pet stores, if they are not common in your area. They make easy-to-care-for class pets.

Hermit crabs use a dead sea snail's empty shell for a home. When they get too big for their present home, they must hunt for a larger one to move into. If you are lucky, this will happen one day in your class. Make sure to provide several appropriately sized shell homes for your pet to choose from.

Turtle Play

Children decorate turtle shells made from paper grocery bags, then use them for turtle play.

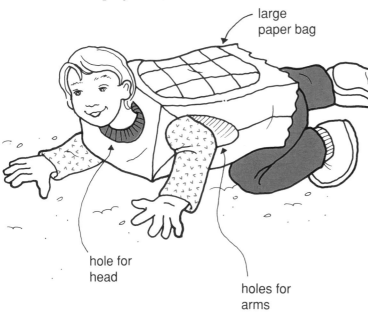

large paper bag

hole for head

holes for arms

On the Bookshelf

Friends help a hermit crab decorate a new and bigger shell home. But soon he outgrows it.

A snail gets his wish for the biggest shell in the world, and learns that biggest is not always best.

A hermit crab searches for a house that fits and will keep him safe from danger.

Fingerplay

This is my turtle. (fist)
He lives in a shell.
He likes his home very well.
He pokes his head out
    (thumb out)
When he wants to eat.
And he pulls it back in
    (thumb in)
When he wants to sleep.

Sharing Experiences

In our mobile society, many students will have already experienced at least one move in their young lives. Some may have immigrated from another country. Many feel a great loss in a move. For all, moving day is a time of excitement and anticipation. Through books and sharing, children can be helped to grow from their experiences.

Encourage children to bring in photographs of homes they once lived in. If you have a large wall map or a globe, take the opportunity to point out the locations of faraway places children may have lived.

Students who have not moved themselves might share an experience in which a best friend moved away.

Why We Moved

My dad got a new job.

My baby sister was born.

We needed a bigger house.

Grandma needed company.

Musical Homes

Pairs of children form houses. Others try to find a home when the music stops.

Goodbye and Hello

Goodbye _____ :
Goodbye _____ :
Goodbye _____ ,
_____ , and _____

Hello _____ .
Hello _____ .
Hello _____ ,
_____ , and _____ .

THEMEWORKS™ : Houses
©1991 Creative Publications

Books about Moving

Making the Move

Children are fascinated by moving vans. If a parent is a mover, take the opportunity to invite him or her to speak to the class about moving —how boxes are packed, how furniture is loaded and unloaded, and so on. Welcome stories about moving day.

Mr. Lee's Visit
Melissa's dad told us a story. It was about the day he found a snake in his moving van. The . . .

Counting Houses

The children can decorate two mathmats from page 52 and use counters on them to model the combinations of ten.

This exceptional book about ten children who move from one house to another can be used as a springboard for some great math activities.

Housewarming

Home Sweet Home

This is the final event in our study of Houses. The event, a Housewarming, centers around the Big House we built over the past days or weeks. (See page 30.) The event provides a way to show off our work and to celebrate its completion. We invite parents, the school principal, and others to join our celebration. And we serve them homemade finger foods and party punch. It all starts with a ribbon-cutting ceremony!

Invitation

Dear_____:

Come to our housewarming party!

Date: _____

Time: _____

Place: _____

I'm glad you could all come to our party.

Balloons are pretty.

THEMEWORKS™ : Houses
©1991 Creative Publications

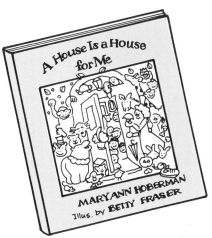

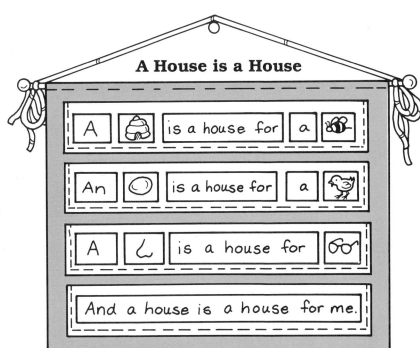

A House is a House

| A | 🍯 | is a house for | a | 🐝 |

| An | ◯ | is a house for | a | 🐤 |

| A | ⌒ | is a house for | 👓 |

| And a house is a house for me. |

This delightful poem about every possible house you can think of opens our minds to creative ways of thinking about what a house really is.

This Is the Way

This is a parody of *Here We Go Round the Mulberry Bush*. Children mimic the actions as we sing.

D
This is the way we dug a hole,

A7
dug a hole, dug a hole.

D
This is the way we dug a hole

A7   D
So early in the morning.

This is the way we hammered the boards,

put up the roof,

painted the house

We can also make up verses for taking care of our house:

· This is the way we sweep the rugs…
· This is the way we wash the windows…
· This is the way we mop the floor…

Songs to Sing: Chants to Chant

This Old Man

Heigh-Ho Merry-O (page 41)

Go In and Out the Window (page 11)

Oh, Do You Know? (page 22)

Hickory Dickory Dock (page 13)

There Was a Crooked Man (page 19)

The Dark House (page 20)

The Goblin (page 21)

The House That Jack Built (page 54)

A Party Game

Pin the
Tail on the
House Mouse

Tell Me a House Riddle

My tail is long,
My coat is brown.
I live in the country
I live in the town.
(a mouse)

I have four legs,
And a back.
But I cannot walk.
(a chair)

I have no legs,
But I can move.
I take my house
Wherever I go.
(a snail)

Peanut Butter Balls

For groups of four:

1. Mix in a bowl:

| ½ cup peanut butter | 1 tablespoon dry milk |
| ½ cup raisins | 1 tablespoon honey |

2. Form into balls.
3. Roll in toppings: coconut, chopped nuts.

Serve with party punch. Mix together different kinds of fruit juices. Serve in a punch bowl.

THEMEWORKS™ : Houses
©1991 Creative Publications

Photo Album

The album displays pictures of the Big House as it is being built by the class. Captions help us remember what happened.

We started with a large box.

We cut out a door and windows.

We added a roof and chimney.

We painted and made decorations.

Now we are ready for a housewarming party.

Categories

Someone names a category and the children give all the examples they can think of. For our study of Houses, the categories could be:

- kinds of houses
- rooms in a house
- parts of a house
- sounds in a house
- house furniture
- construction workers
- construction tools
- people who live in a house
- animal homes
- house pets

House • Outside View

THEMEWORKS™ : Houses
©1991 Creative Publications

House • Inside View

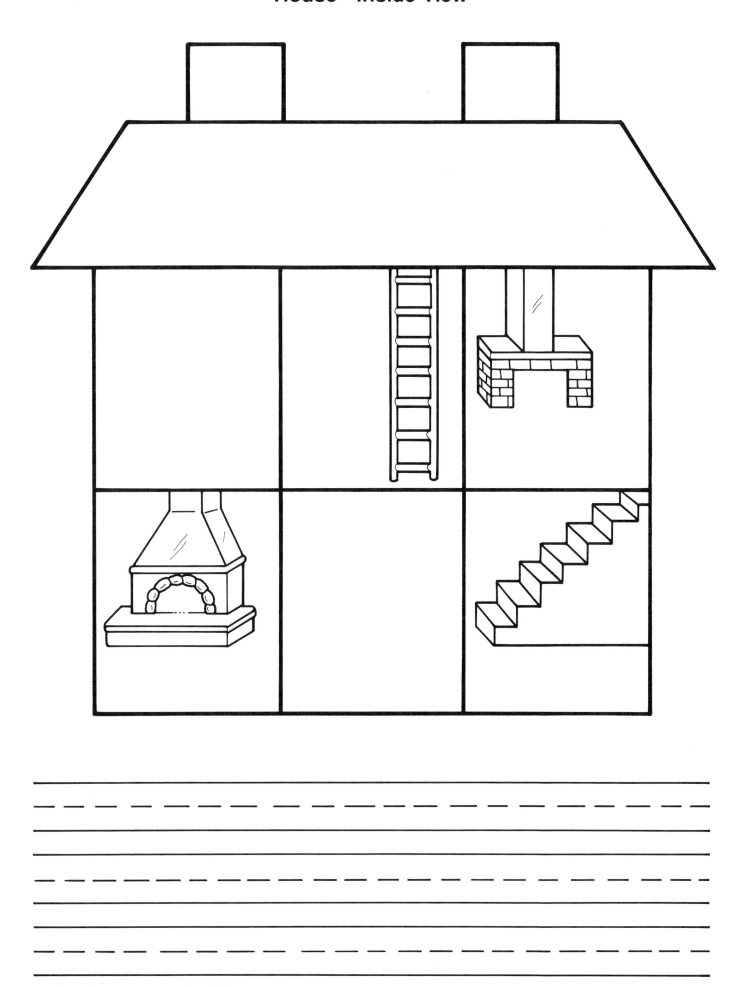

THEMEWORKS™ : Houses

The House That Jack Built

This is the house that Jack built.

This is the malt that lay in the house that Jack built.

This is the rat that ate the malt that lay in the house that Jack built.

This is the cat that killed the rat that ate the malt that lay in the house that Jack built.

This is the dog that worried the cat that killed the rat that ate the malt that lay in the house that Jack built.

This is the cow with the crumpled horn, that tossed the dog that worried the cat that killed the rat that ate the malt that lay in the house that Jack built.

This is the maiden all forlorn, that milked the cow with the crumpled horn, that tossed the dog that worried the cat that killed the rat that ate the malt that lay in the house that Jack built.

This is the man all tattered and torn, that kissed the maiden all forlorn, that milked the cow with the crumpled horn, that tossed the dog that worried the cat that killed the rat that ate the malt that lay in the house that Jack built.

This is the priest all shaven and shorn, that married the man all tattered and torn, that kissed the maiden all forlorn, that milked the cow with the crumpled horn, that tossed the dog that worried the cat that killed the rat that ate the malt that lay in the house that Jack built.

This is the cock that crowed in the morn, that waked the priest all shaven and shorn, that married the man all tattered and torn, that kissed the maiden all forlorn, that milked the cow with the crumpled horn, that tossed the dog that worried the cat that killed the rat that ate the malt that lay in the house that Jack built.

This is the farmer sowing the corn, that kept the cock that crowed in the morn, that waked the priest all shaven and shorn, that married the man all tattered and torn, that kissed the maiden all forlorn, that milked the cow with the crumpled horn, that tossed the dog that worried the cat that killed the rat that ate the malt that lay in the house that Jack built.

Animal Cards

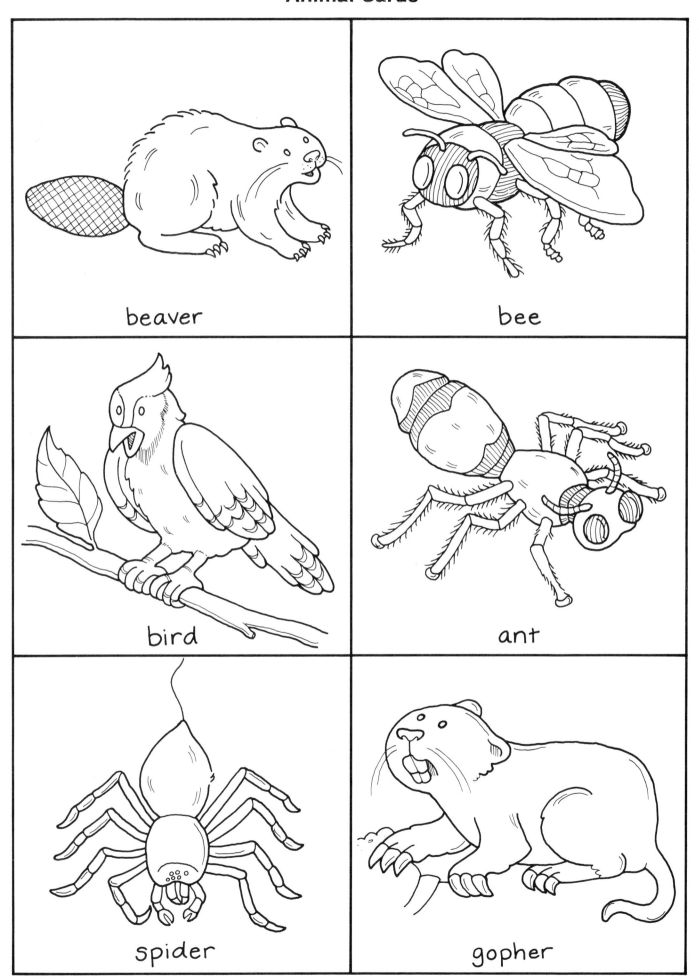

beaver

bee

bird

ant

spider

gopher

THEMEWORKS™ : Houses
©1991 Creative Publications

Animal Home Cards

hive

lodge

hill

nest

hole

web

THEMEWORKS™ : Houses
©1991 Creative Publications

Word Cards

house	roof	chimney
window	door	wall
garage	driveway	yard
sidewalk	fence	porch
deck	kitchen	hall
bathroom	living room	bedroom
dining room	playroom	basement

Curriculum Chart

	Language	Mathematics	Science	Social Studies	Art	Cooking	Music/Movement	P.E.	Dramatic
House Ramble pp. 10 - 11	• labeling • poem	• shapes • tallies • patterns					• song	• singing game	
House Mouse pp. 12 - 13	• storybook • writing • poem • nursery rhyme • phonics	• clock time • counting		• town vs. country	• drawing		• song	• cat and mouse game	
Look Inside pp. 14 - 15	• fingerplay • labels • storybook • language frame	• numbers • addition			• dioramas				
Home Is a Special Place pp. 16 - 17	• poems • storybook • frames	• number • graphing • shapes	• five senses	• feelings	• drawing				
House Fantasies pp. 18 - 19	• storybooks • frames • invitation • poem	• shapes			• shape collage		• song		

THEMEWORKS™ : Houses
©1991 Creative Publications

Curriculum Chart

	Language	Mathematics	Science	Social Studies	Art	Cooking	Music/Movement	P.E.	Dramatic Play
Monsters in the House pp. 20 - 21	• storybooks • chant • experience chart • class book • poem	• graph • survey		• fears	• drawings		• song	• pantomiming actions	
Where Do You Live? pp. 22 - 23	• writing	• number order • buying		• street names • addresses • occupations	• drawing		• song	• movement game	• mail carrier
Long Ago and Far Away pp. 24 - 25	• storybooks • fill-in story • poem • fairy tales			• homes around the world • homes long ago	• sand castle construction		• song		
Under Construction pp. 26 - 27	• captions	• sequence • shapes		• occupations • maps	• printing • construction • photography				
The House That We Build pp. 28 - 29	• rhyme • experience chart • writing • thank-you note	• prices • length • weight	• physical knowledge	• workers	• drawing				• hardware store

Curriculum Chart

	Language	Mathematics	Science	Social Studies	Art	Cooking	Music/Movement	P.E.	Dramatic Play
The Big House pp. 30 - 31	• storybook	• problem solving • time • sharing • following a sequence	• pulley	• workers • cooperation	• hat construction	• egg salad			• construction site
Knock, Knock, Who's There? pp. 32 - 33	• poem	• graph • voting		• the family	• portraits			• Mother May I?	• the family
House Tales pp. 34 - 35	• folktales • chant • experience chart • reading	• shapes • number • halves/wholes	• physical knowledge		• house decorating • construction • finger puppets	• ginger house cookies			• puppetry
They Lived in a Shoe pp. 36 - 37	• nursery rhyme • storybook • poem	• number • sorting • graphing			• pipe cleaner children	• broth			
The Three Bears pp. 38 - 39	• storybook • storytelling • frame reading	• ordering by size • measurement				• porridge			• story acting

THEMEWORKS™ : Houses
©1991 Creative Publications

Curriculum Chart

	Language	Mathematics	Science	Social Studies	Art	Cooking	Music/Movement	P.E.	Dramatic Play
Animal Homes pp. 40 - 41	• frame writing • poem		• animal homes	• reference books	• drawing		• song	• pantomime	
I Spy pp. 42 - 43	• poetry book • poem	• tallies	• animal homes	• animal needs					
Home in a Shell pp. 44 - 45	• storybooks • fingerplay	• sorting • ordering • comparing • number • measurement	• animal homes		• turtle costume • snails	• baker's dough			• turtles
On the Move pp. 46 - 47	• storybooks • language frames • experience charts	• addition combinations		• shared experiences • map readiness • workers			• recordings	• musical homes	
House-warming pp. 48 - 51	• invitation • poem • riddles			• categories		• peanut butter balls • punch	• songs		

Resource List

Stories

Ahlberg, Allan and Janet. *The Jolly Postman*. Boston: Little, Brown, 1986.

Anno, Mitsumasa. *Anno's Counting House*. New York: Philomel, 1982.

Carle, Eric. *A House for Hermit Crab*. Saxonville, MA: Picture Book Studio, 1987.

Christiansen, C.B. *My Mother's House, My Father's House*. New York: Atheneum, 1989.

Clark, Ann Nolan. *In My Mother's House*. New York: Viking, 1941.

deRegniers, Beatrice Schenk. *A Little House of Your Own*. New York: Harcourt Brace, 1954.

Duvoisin, Roger. *The House of Four Seasons*. New York: Lothrop, Lee and Shepard, 1956.

Falconer, Elizabeth. *The House That Jack Built: A rebus book*. Nashville: Ideals Children's Books, 1990.

Gackenbach, Dick. *Harry and the Terrible Whatzit*. New York: Seabury, 1977.

Grifalconi, Ann. *The Village of Round and Square Houses*. Boston: Little, Brown, 1986.

Hill, Elizabeth Starr. *Evan's Corner*. New York: Holt, Rinehart and Winston, 1967.

Hoberman, Mary Ann. *A House is a House for Me*. New York: Viking, 1978.

Hughes, Shirley. *Moving Molly*. New York: Prentice-Hall, 1978.

_____. *Sally's Secret*. New York: Viking, 1973.

Isadora, Rachel. *The Potters' Kitchen*. New York: Greenwillow Books, 1978.

Johnston, Tony. *The Quilt Story*. New York: Putnam, 1985.

Keats, Ezra Jack. *The Trip*. New York: Greenwillow Books, 1978.

Komaiko, Leah. *Annie Bananie*. New York: Harper and Row, 1987.

Krauss, Ruth. *A Very Special House*. New York: Harper and Row, 1953.

Leodhas, Sorche Nic. *Always Room for One More*. New York: Holt, Rinehart and Winston, 1965.

Lionni, Leo. *Alexander and the Wind-up Mouse*. New York: Pantheon, 1969.

_____. *The Biggest House in the World*. New York: Pantheon, 1968.

Mayer, Mercer. *There's a Nightmare in My Closet*. New York: Dial, 1968.

_____. *There's an Alligator Under My Bed*. New York: Dial, 1987.

Maynard, Joyce. *New House*. New York: Harcourt Brace, 1987.

McDonald, Megan. *Is This a House for a Hermit Crab?* Granville, OH: Orchard, 1990.

O'Donnell, Elizabeth Lee. *Maggie Doesn't Want to Move*. New York: Four Winds Press, 1987.

Peppe, Rodney. *The Mice Who Lived in a Shoe*. New York: Lothrop, Lee and Shepard, 1981.

Rockwell, Anne. *In Our House*. New York: Thomas Y. Crowell, 1985.

Schlein, Miriam. *My House*. Niles, IL: Albert Whitman, and Co. 1971.

Turkle, Brinton. *Deep in the Forest*. New York: E. P. Dutton, 1976.

Waber, Bernard. *Ira Says Goodbye*. Boston: Houghton Mifflin, 1988.

Watson, Wendy. *Moving*. New York: Thomas Y. Crowell, 1978.

Zalinsky, Paul O. *The Maid and the Mouse and the Odd-Shaped House*. New York: Dodd, Mead and Co. 1981.

Zolotow, Charlotte. *Janey*. New York: Harper and Row, 1973.

Fairy Tales, Folktales, and Legends

Galdone, Paul. *The Three Bears*. Boston: Houghton Mifflin, 1972.

_____. *The Three Little Pigs*. Boston: Houghton Mifflin, 1970.

Grimm. *Hansel and Gretel* (retold by Rika Lesser). New York: Putnam, 1984.

_____. *Hansel and Gretel* (retold by Susan Jeffers). New York: Dial Press, 1980.

Marshall, James. *The Three Pigs*. New York: Dial Books for Young Readers, 1989.

Nonfiction

Barton, Byron. *Building a House*. New York: Greenwillow Books, 1981.

George, William T. and Lindsay Barrett. *Beaver at Long Pond*. New York: Greenwillow Books, 1988.

Gibbons, Gail. *The Post Office Book*. New York: Thomas Y. Crowell, 1982.

Macaulay, David. *Castle*. Boston: Houghton Mifflin, 1977.

Reyes, Gregg and Judy Hindley. *Once There Was a House and you can make it!* New York: Random House, 1987.

Robbins, Ken. *Building a House*. New York: Four Winds Press, 1984.

Rockwell, Anne and Harlow. *The Toolbox*. New York: The Macmillan Co., 1971.

Rowland-Entwistle, Theodore. *Animal Homes*. New York: Random House,1978.

Wildsmith, Brian. *Animal Homes*. Oxford Univ. Press, 1980.

National Geographic magazines

National Geographic World magazines

Ranger Rick magazines

Poetry Anthologies

Fisher, Aileen. *Anybody Home?* New York: Thomas Y. Crowell, 1980.

Frasconi, Antonio. *The House That Jack Built: A Picture Book in Two Languages*. New York: Harcourt Brace, 1958.

Mizumura, Kazue. *If I Built a Village*. New York: Thomas Y. Crowell, 1971.

Stevens, Janet. *The House That Jack Built*. New York: Holiday House, 1985.

Songs

A Tisket, A Tasket

Go Round and Round the Village

Hickory Dickory Dock

There Was a Crooked Man

Acknowledgements

Grateful acknowledgement is made to the following for permission to reprint their copyrighted material. Every reasonable effort has been made to trace the ownership of all copyrighted material included in this book. Any errors which may have occurred are inadvertent and will be corrected in subsequent editions, provided notification is sent to the publisher.

Aileen Fisher "Houses" from UP THE WINDY HILL. Copyright © 1953 Abelard, renewed 1981. Reprinted by permission of Aileen Fisher.

Rose Fyleman "Mice" from FIFTY-ONE NEW NURSERY RHYMES by Rose Fyleman. Copyright © 1931, 1932 by Doubleday, a division of Bantam, Doubleday, Dell Publishing Group, Inc. Used by permission of the publisher.

Rose Fyleman "A Goblin Lives in Our House" adapted from SUGAR AND SPICE, edited by Rose Fyleman. Reprinted by permission of Western Publishing Company, Inc.

Lucy Sprague Mitchell "The House of the Mouse" from ANOTHER HERE AND NOW STORYBOOK by Lucy Sprague Mitchell. Copyright © 1937 E.P. Dutton and Co., Inc., renewed 1965 by Lucy Sprague Mitchell. Used by permission of Dutton Children's Books, a division of Penguin Books, USA Inc.

Jack Prelutsky "Home! You're Where It's Warm Inside" from THE RANDOM HOUSE BOOK OF POETRY FOR CHILDREN, selected and introduced by Jack Prelutsky. Copyright © 1983 by Random House, Inc.

Marci Ridlon "Castles," copyright © 1969 by Marci Ridlon. Used by permission of the author.

Dorothy Brown Thompson "Our House" Reprinted from *Child Life Magazine*. Copyright reassigned to Dorothy Brown Thompson. Reprinted by permission of Dorothy Brown Thompson.

Bev Veitch and Thelma Harms "Three Bear Porridge" from COOK AND LEARN by Bev Veitch and Thelma Harms. Copyright © 1981 by Addison-Wesley Publishing Co. Reprinted by permission of Addison-Wesley.

Judith Viorst "Mother Doesn't Want a Dog" from IF I WERE IN CHARGE OF THE WORLD AND OTHER WORRIES by Judith Viorst. Copyright © 1981 by Judith Viorst. Reprinted with permission of Atheneum Publishers, an imprint of Macmillan Publishing Company.